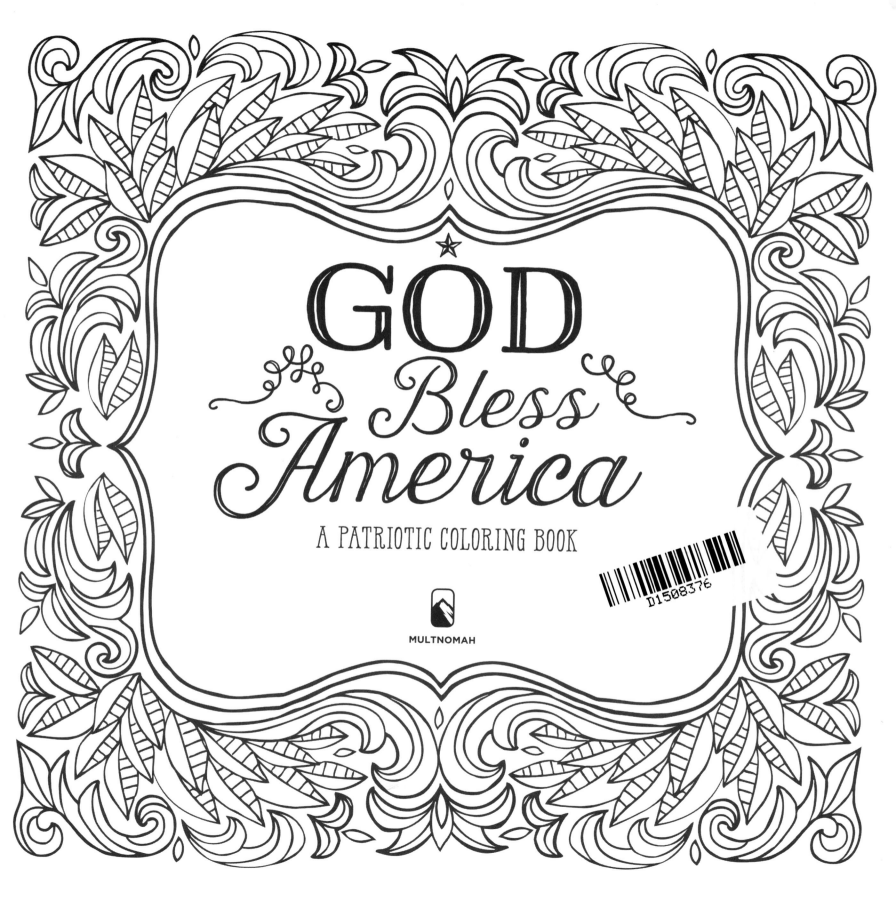

GOD Bless America

A PATRIOTIC COLORING BOOK

MULTNOMAH

GOD BLESS AMERICA

All Scripture quotations, unless otherwise indicated, are taken from the Holy Bible, New International Version®, NIV®. Copyright © 1973, 1978, 1984 by Biblica Inc®. Used by permission. All rights reserved worldwide. Scripture quotations marked (KJV) are taken from the King James Version.

All songs and hymns quoted are in the public domain.

Trade Paperback ISBN 978-0-7352-8974-1

Copyright © 2016 by Multnomah

Cover design by Kristopher K. Orr; cover image by Jennifer Tucker

Published in the United States by Multnomah, an imprint of the Crown Publishing Group, a division of Penguin Random House LLC, New York.

MULTNOMAH® and its mountain colophon are registered trademarks of Penguin Random House LLC.

Printed in the United States of America
2016—First Edition

10 9 8 7 6 5 4 3 2 1

SPECIAL SALES
Most Multnomah books are available at special quantity discounts when purchased in bulk by corporations, organizations, and special-interest groups. Custom imprinting or excerpting can also be done to fit special needs. For information, please e-mail specialmarketscms@penguinrandomhouse.com or call 1-800-603-7051.

Celebrate America's Colorful History

America is a nation of dreamers, world changers, and creative thinkers. Founded on the principles of life, liberty, and the pursuit of happiness, our nation is strongest when we are united. Sometimes, though, it's easy to become caught up in the troubles we face as a nation—war, economic strife, political discord, social discontent. But as Adlai Stevenson so appropriately stated, "If America ever loses confidence in herself, she will retain the confidence of no one, and she will lose her chance to be free, because the fearful are never free."

The fearful are never free.

That is why we created this coloring book—to take you from fear into quiet reflection on God's sovereignty over our nation. Coloring can't change the world, but it can help change your perspective. As you color these patriotic images, take the time to reflect on the quotes from our Founding Fathers, historic documents, presidents, Scripture, patriotic songs, and inspirational quotes from America's heroes. Take the time to mull over what makes America a truly amazing country—our values of equality, opportunity, faith, family, character, generosity, justice, and perseverance.

Use this book to help quiet your mind as you spend time with God, use it to help you relax after a long day of working, or use it to simply find a unique outlet for your creativity. Ultimately, let it remind you how blessed we are to live in a nation as extraordinary as the United States of America, and let the words of the patriots from American history inspire you to help keep this country amazing. And if you Instagram any of your coloring pages, we'd love it if you could hashtag them with #ColoringAmerica.

A link to a Spotify playlist called "Coloring America" is at the back of this book. As you color, have it playing in the background to enhance your patriotic experience.

We hope that as you take the time to color and reflect on our nation's history, its present, its future, and all the ways the Almighty has carefully guided our country, you will be inspired to live out the words of George Washington from his farewell address, "Observe good faith and justice towards all nations; cultivate peace and harmony with all."

And may God bless America.

#ColoringAmerica

"Where liberty dwells, there is my country." —Benjamin Franklin

Benjamin Franklin (1706–1790) wrote these words in 1773 in a letter to his British friend Benjamin Vaughan, a participant in the negotiations for peace between England and the United States.

Franklin is best known as one of the Founding Fathers who drafted and signed the Declaration of Independence. He was also a member of the Continental Congress and a signer of the United States Constitution.

Benjamin Franklin is one of the most notable individuals in our nation's history. In addition to his accomplishments as a civic leader, diplomat, and statesman, he was a writer, printer, publisher, philosopher, humorist, scientist, and inventor. His inventions were as diverse as the topics he studied and include the lightning rod, bifocals, swim fins, the odometer, the urinary catheter, and the Franklin stove. He also was instrumental in furthering our understanding of electricity and the movement of ocean currents.

In 1732, Benjamin Franklin published the first *Poor Richard's Almanack,* which contained many proverbs and idioms forever tied to Franklin, such as "Early to bed and early to rise, makes a man healthy, wealthy, and wise"; "Well done is better than well said"; and "Fish and visitors smell after three days."

Illustrated and hand-lettered by Holly Camp

The Star-Spangled Banner
by Francis Scott Key

Oh, say, can you see, by the dawn's early light,
What so proudly we hail'd at the twilight's last gleaming?
Whose broad stripes and bright stars, thro' the perilous fight,
O'er the ramparts we watch'd, were so gallantly streaming?

And the rockets' red glare, the bombs bursting in air,
Gave proof thro' the night that our flag was still there.
O say, does that star-spangled banner yet wave
O'er the land of the free and the home of the brave?

At the sight of the American flag still flying over Fort McHenry in Baltimore, Maryland—after a twenty-five-hour bombardment by British forces—Francis Scott Key penned these lines on the back of a letter while trying to secure the release of a friend held captive aboard a British ship. This poem, written on September 14, 1814, became the first verse of "The Star-Spangled Banner" and propelled the flag into prominence as an expression of patriotism, endurance, and courage. A congressional resolution in 1931, signed by President Herbert Hoover, officially designated "The Star-Spangled Banner" as our national anthem.

Illustrated by Christina J. Culver

The phrase "In God We Trust" made its appearance on our currency by an Act of Congress in 1864. When the motto was omitted from new gold coins in 1907, public uproar resulted in a law that made "In God We Trust" mandatory on all coins on which it had previously appeared. Legislation approved on July 11, 1955, made "In God We Trust" mandatory on all US coins and paper currency.

President Dwight D. Eisenhower signed into law the declaration "In God We Trust" as the nation's official motto on July 30, 1956.

Illustrated and hand-lettered by Jennifer Tucker

Liberties are the
gift of God.

—Thomas Jefferson

"God who gave us life gave us liberty. Can the liberties of a nation be secure when we have removed a conviction that these liberties are the gift of God? Indeed I tremble for my country when I reflect that God is just, that his justice cannot sleep forever." —Thomas Jefferson

These words, which originated in "A Summary View of the Rights of British America" and the *Notes on the State of Virginia,* Query XVIII, are inscribed on the Jefferson Memorial in Washington, DC.

Founding Father Thomas Jefferson (1743–1826)—author of the Declaration of Independence and the Virginia Statute for Religious Freedom—became the third president of the United States and founder of the University of Virginia. He was also responsible for the Louisiana Purchase.

At age twenty-six, Jefferson began designing Monticello (his Virginia home shown in the illustration) and spent more than four decades building, dismantling, redesigning, and rebuilding his estate. He died at Monticello on July 4, 1826.

Illustrated by Melinda B. Shiflet

"I pledge allegiance to the flag of the United States of America, and to the republic for which it stands, one nation under God, indivisible, with liberty and justice for all." —Pledge of Allegiance

The Pledge of Allegiance, as written in August 1892 by minister Francis Bellamy, originally said, "I pledge allegiance to my Flag and the Republic for which it stands, one nation, indivisible, with liberty and justice for all." In 1923 and 1924, "to my Flag" was replaced with "to the flag of the United States of America." The pledge was formally recognized by Congress in 1942. In 1943, the Supreme Court ruled that no person can be required to recite the pledge. In 1954, President Dwight D. Eisenhower urged Congress to add "under God," and this change to our current pledge was adopted on Flag Day that year.

Illustrated by Bridget Hurley
Hand-lettered by Jennifer Tucker

"Wars may be fought with weapons, but they are won by men. It is the spirit of the men who follow and of the man who leads that gains the victory."
—George S. Patton, one of the greatest combat generals in US history

General George S. Patton (1885–1945) was especially skilled at mobile tank warfare. He served as a captain, then lieutenant colonel, in the Tank Corps in World War I. Badly wounded by a machine gun bullet, he refused to be transported to the hospital until he had reported to his commander. He was awarded the Distinguished Service Cross for bravery under fire in 1918.

Patton, who was both complex and contradictory, was promoted to general during World War II. He helped lead the Allies to victory in the invasion of Sicily, and he was instrumental in the liberation of Germany from the Nazis. A colorful character who was widely admired by the men who served under him, he earned the nickname "Old Blood and Guts." Patton died in Heidelberg, Germany, in 1945 as a result of a broken neck suffered in an auto accident.

Illustrated by Christina J. Culver

Preservation of one's own culture does not require contempt or disrespect for other's cultures. —Cesar Chavez

"Preservation of one's own culture does not require contempt or disrespect for other cultures." —Cesar Chavez, founder of the National Farm Workers Association, which later became the United Farm Workers

As a labor leader, Cesar Chavez (1927–1993) brought attention to the plight of farmworkers through such nonviolent means as marches and boycotts. He was willing to sacrifice his own life for those in the union by going on hunger strikes for weeks or more at a time, as a way to bring attention to the suffering of farmworkers and their children, their lack of rights, and the dangers they faced because of exposure to pesticides. For thirty years, this Mexican-American icon devoted himself to trying to improve the situations of some of the poorest workers in America.

Illustrated and hand-lettered by Lisa Shirk

"The clash of ideas is the sound of freedom."
—Claudia Alta Taylor "Lady Bird" Johnson

Lady Bird Johnson (1912–2007), wife of President Lyndon B. Johnson, was the First Lady of the United States from 1963 to 1969. Lady Bird is considered one of the most influential and important first ladies. She was an environmentalist who advocated for the beautification of cities and highways. The Beautification Act of 1965 was one result of Mrs. Johnson's efforts. This act called for control of outdoor advertising, including the removal of certain types of signs along the nation's Interstates. It also required junkyards along Interstates and primary highways to be removed or screened and encouraged other scenic enhancements along roadsides.

In 1977, Lady Bird Johnson was awarded the Presidential Medal of Freedom by Gerald Ford. She then received the Congressional Gold Medal from President Ronald Regan in 1988, becoming the first wife of a president to receive it.

In 1982, Mrs. Johnson founded the National Wildflower Research Center, a non-profit environmental organization dedicated to the preservation and reestablishment of native plants in natural and planned landscapes.

Mrs. Johnson passed away in 2007, the first former First Lady to die in the twenty-first century.

Illustrated and hand-lettered by Holly Camp

My Country, 'Tis of Thee
by Samuel Francis Smith

My country, 'tis of thee,
Sweet land of liberty,
Of thee I sing;
Land where my fathers died,
Land of the pilgrims' pride,
From every mountainside
Let freedom ring!

My native country, thee,
Land of the noble free,
Thy name I love;
I love thy rocks and rills,
Thy woods and templed hills;
My heart with rapture thrills,
Like that above.

Let music swell the breeze,
And ring from all the trees,
Sweet freedom's song;
Let mortal tongues awake;
Let all that breathe partake;
Let rocks their silence break,
The sound prolong.

Our fathers' God, to Thee,
Author of liberty,
To Thee we sing;
Long may our land be bright
With freedom's holy light;
Protect us by Thy might,
Great God, our King.

Baptist pastor Samuel Francis Smith composed the lyrics to this American patriotic hymn in 1831 on a scrap of paper in a half-hour's time. This song, unchanged from the original scrap of paper version, was often used as a national anthem until "The Star-Spangled Banner" became the official anthem in 1931.

Illustrated by Deborah Gregg

"Whoever oppresses the poor shows contempt for their Maker,
    but whoever is kind to the needy honors God.
When calamity comes, the wicked are brought down,
    but even in death the righteous seek refuge in God.
Wisdom reposes in the heart of the discerning
    and even among fools she lets herself be known.
Righteousness exalts a nation,
    but sin condemns any people." —Proverbs 14:31–34

Illustrated and hand-lettered by Bridget Hurley

"The British are coming!"

These are the words often attributed to Paul Revere (1735–1818) on his midnight horse-back ride to Lexington, Massachusetts, to warn Samuel Adams and John Hancock of the approach of the British to arrest them on April 18, 1775. But Revere didn't gain fame during his lifetime for carrying this message—in fact, he never even shouted these words. He would have carried the message quietly (and he likely would have called them "the regulars"—the term then used for British soldiers) because his spying was done discreetly so as not to alert British soldiers hiding along the countryside. It was Henry Wadsworth Longfellow's poem "Midnight Ride" in 1861 that etched this phrase and Paul Revere's ride in history.

Illustrated by Joseph Marsh

Proclaim liberty throughout all the land unto all the inhabitants thereof. —Leviticus 25:10 (KJV)

"Proclaim liberty throughout all the land unto all the inhabitants thereof." —Leviticus 25:10 (KJV)

This verse, from the King James Version, is inscribed on the Liberty Bell. The bell, originally called the State House bell, was created in 1751 to commemorate the fiftieth anniversary of Pennsylvania's original constitution, William Penn's Charter of Privileges. Abolitionists who later adopted the bell as a symbol in their effort to end slavery named it "Liberty Bell" in 1835. After the Civil War, both the American flag and the Liberty Bell became iconic symbols of unity and independence in the fractured country.

Illustrated by Melinda B. Shiflet

"I am certain that my fellow Americans expect that on my induction into the Presidency I will address them with a candor and a decision which the present situation of our people impel. This is preeminently the time to speak the truth, the whole truth, frankly and boldly. Nor need we shrink from honestly facing conditions in our country today. This great Nation will endure as it has endured, will revive and will prosper. So, first of all, let me assert my firm belief that the only thing we have to fear is fear itself— nameless, unreasoning, unjustified terror which paralyzes needed efforts to convert retreat into advance. In every dark hour of our national life a leadership of frankness and vigor has met with that understanding and support of the people themselves which is essential to victory. I am convinced that you will again give that support to leadership in these critical days." —President Franklin D. Roosevelt

These are the opening words spoken by Franklin D. Roosevelt (1882–1945) in his first inaugural address in 1933, at the depths of the Great Depression.

Roosevelt was the thirty-second president of the United States, the only US president to be elected to serve four terms. He died of a stroke three months into his fourth term in office.

Illustrated and hand-lettered by Jennifer Tucker

"We must all learn to live together as brothers—or we will all perish together as fools." —Martin Luther King Jr.

Dr. Martin Luther King Jr. (1929–1968) spoke these words in a commencement address to Oberlin College in June 1965.

King, a Baptist minister who dedicated his life to achieving equality and justice for Americans of all races, fought against the legal segregation of African Americans, particularly in the South. He played a pivotal role in the passing of the Civil Rights Act of 1964, which required equal access to public places and employment; enforced desegregation of schools; and outlawed discrimination on the basis of race, color, religion, sex, or national origin. He was awarded the Nobel Peace Prize the same year. Dr. King was assassinated by James Earl Ray in 1968.

Illustrated and hand-lettered by Lisa Shirk

America the Beautiful
by Katharine Lee Bates

O beautiful for spacious skies,
For amber waves of grain,
For purple mountain majesties
Above the fruited plain!
America! America! God shed His grace on thee,
And crown thy good with brotherhood
From sea to shining sea!

O beautiful for pilgrim feet,
Whose stern impassion'd stress
A thoroughfare for freedom beat
Across the wilderness!
America! America! God mend thine ev'ry flaw,
Confirm thy soul in self-control,
Thy liberty in law!

O beautiful for heroes proved In liberating strife,
Who more than self their country loved,
And mercy more than life!
America! America! May God thy gold refine
Till all success be nobleness,
And ev'ry gain divine!

O Beautiful for patriot dream
That sees beyond the years
Thine alabaster cities gleam,
Undimmed by human tears!
America! America! God shed His grace on thee,
And crown thy good with brotherhood
From sea to shining sea!

In 1893, Katharine Lee Bates (1859–1929), a poet and professor at Wellesley College in Massachusetts, was in Colorado Springs to teach a summer course at Colorado College. She and her colleagues decided to travel by prairie wagon to the top of Pikes Peak to celebrate the end of the summer session. She was so awestruck by the view from the peak that she composed this poem, which later became one of the best known songs in American history.

Illustrated and hand-lettered by Holly Camp

In no other land could a boy from a country village... look forward with unbounded hope.

—HERBERT HOOVER

"My country owes me nothing. It gave me, as it gives
every boy and girl, a chance. It gave me schooling,
independence of action, opportunity for service and
honor. In no other land could a boy from a country village,
without inheritance or influential friends, look forward
with unbounded hope." —Herbert Hoover

Herbert Hoover wrote this in a letter to the chairman of the Republican national convention, upon learning of his presidential nomination in June 1928.

Herbert Hoover (1874–1964) was known as "The Great Humanitarian" because of his role in feeding war-torn Belgium during and after World War I, when he served as the head of the US Food Administration under President Wilson.

Within months of beginning his presidency in 1929, the stock market crashed and the Great Depression began. Even though the policies of his predecessors also contributed to the economic downfall, President Hoover was the scapegoat and was soundly defeated in 1932 by Franklin D. Roosevelt.

Illustrated by Deborah Gregg

"In the long history of the world, only a few generations have been granted the role of defending freedom in its hour of maximum danger. I do not shrink from this responsibility—I welcome it. I do not believe that any of us would exchange places with any other people or any other generation. The energy, the faith, the devotion which we bring to this endeavour will light our country and all who serve it—and the glow from that fire can truly light the world.

"And so, my fellow Americans: ask not what your country can do for you—ask what you can do for your country.

"My fellow citizens of the world: ask not what America will do for you, but what together we can do for the freedom of man.

"Finally, whether you are citizens of America or citizens of the world, ask of us the same high standards of strength and sacrifice which we ask of you. With a good conscience our only sure reward, with history the final judge of our deeds, let us go forth to lead the land we love, asking His blessing and His help, but knowing that here on earth God's work must truly be our own."
—President John F. Kennedy

President John F. Kennedy (1917–1963) concluded his inauguration speech with these words on January 20, 1961. Kennedy, often referred to as JFK, was the youngest man—and the first Roman Catholic—ever elected president (although Teddy Roosevelt was the youngest to ever *serve* as president; he was appointed after McKinley's assassination). President Kennedy was assassinated on November 22, 1963, which also made him the youngest president to die. Despite the numerous international crises that JFK faced during his presidency, there were also bright spots: the Nuclear Test-Ban Treaty, the Alliance for Progress, advancements in the space program, and the establishment of the Peace Corps all occurred during his years in office.

Illustrated by Bridget Hurley
Hand-lettered by Jennifer Tucker

I may be compelled
to face danger,
but never fear it,
and while our
soldiers can stand and fight,
I can stand and feed
and nurse them.

—Clara Barton

"I may be compelled to face danger, but never fear it, and while our soldiers can stand and fight, I can stand and feed and nurse them." —Clara Barton, the "Angel of the Battlefield"

Clara Barton (1821–1912), a US Patent Office clerk, risked her life by aiding Civil War soldiers who lacked supplies and food. She gathered necessary items and delivered them to the front lines of battle. She was later permitted to ride in army ambulances to nurse wounded soldiers and assist doctors operating on injured soldiers.

After the war, President Lincoln appointed her to assist the families of missing soldiers. She created the Office of the Friends of Missing Soldiers for this purpose, and she located over twenty-two thousand missing soldiers over a period of three years.

In 1881, Barton established the American Association of the Red Cross to assist in future crises where medical assistance and supplies were needed. She served as president of the Red Cross until 1904.

Illustrated by Christina J. Culver

A FREE GOVERNMENT SERVICE
GRAND CANYON
NATIONAL   PARK
U.S. DEPARTMENT   NATIONAL PARK
OF THE INTERIOR   SERVICE

Over eighty-four million acres of prized and sacred land in our country is protected and preserved for the enjoyment of American citizens and visitors, thanks to "America's Best Idea"—the National Park System.

The founding of the National Park System began with the 1872 congressional act establishing Yellowstone National Park as a public park for the benefit of the people. In 1916, the Organic Act was approved by Congress to establish a National Park Service under the Department of the Interior. Public land throughout the country has been set aside as national parks "to conserve the scenery and the natural and historic objects and the wild life therein and to…leave them unimpaired for the enjoyment of future generations."

Not only did Yellowstone inspire our own National Park System, now more than one hundred countries across the globe have national parks or equivalents.

Illustrated by Joseph Marsh

It isn't enough to talk of peace.
One must believe it. And it isn't enough
to believe in it. One must work at it.

—Eleanor Roosevelt

"It isn't enough to talk of peace. One must
believe it. And it isn't enough to believe in it.
One must work at it." —Eleanor Roosevelt

Americans heard these words from First Lady Eleanor Roosevelt (1884–1962) during
a *Voice of America* broadcast on November 11, 1951.

Mrs. Roosevelt, the wife of Franklin D. Roosevelt, was the longest-serving First
Lady in history. She filled that role from 1933 until her husband's death in office in
1945. Her active participation in politics was a first for a president's wife, and as a
result changed the role of First Lady for the generations that followed. Eleanor, a
leader of women's and civil rights, was one of the first public officials to use mass
media to discuss important issues.

Illustrated by Melinda B. Shiflet

"Independence is happiness." —Susan B. Anthony

Abolitionist and women's rights leader Susan B. Anthony (1820–1906) was an agent for the American Anti-Slavery Society from 1856 until the Civil War. She dedicated her post–Civil War life to women's right to vote. After cofounding the National Woman Suffrage Association in 1869, she spoke around the country about this cause. Susan and fourteen other women illegally voted in the 1872 presidential election, for which she was arrested and fined. It wasn't until fourteen years after her death that the Nineteenth Amendment to the Constitution was passed, ensuring the right of all women to vote. In 1979, one-dollar coins with Susan B. Anthony's portrait were issued by the Treasury Department, making her the first woman to appear on US currency.

Illustrated and hand-lettered by Bridget Hurley

Let us *die* to make men *free.*

—Julia Ward Howe

The Battle Hymn of the Republic
by Julia Ward Howe

Mine eyes have seen the glory of the coming of the Lord;
He is trampling out the vintage where the grapes of wrath are stored;
He hath loosed the fateful lightning of His terrible swift sword,
His truth is marching on.

Chorus:
Glory, glory, hallelujah! Glory, glory, hallelujah!
Glory, glory, hallelujah! His truth is marching on.

I have seen Him in the watchfires of a hundred circling camps;
They have builded Him an altar in the evening dews and damps;
I can read His righteous sentence by the dim and flaring lamps,
His day is marching on.
Chorus

He has sounded forth the trumpet that shall never call retreat;
He is sifting out the hearts of men before His Judgement Seat.
Oh! Be swift, my soul, to answer Him, be jubilant, my feet!
Our God is marching on.
Chorus

In the beauty of the lilies Christ was born across the sea,
With a glory in His bosom that transfigures you and me;
As He died to make men holy, let us die to make men free,
While God is marching on.
Chorus

Late in 1861, poet and abolitionist Julia Ward Howe (1819–1910) was visiting Union army camps with her husband and their friend Reverend James Freeman Clarke. They watched as troops marched away singing Civil War songs, including a distressing one called "John Brown's Body," about a man who had been hanged for attempting to help slaves. Reverend Clarke suggested that Mrs. Howe create better lyrics to this familiar tune, a challenge she heartily embraced. The words to one of the finest patriotic songs, "The Battle Hymn of the Republic," formed in her head as she awoke the next morning.

Illustrated by Katherine Howe

"One and God make a majority." —Frederick Douglass

Frederick Augustus Washington Bailey (circa 1818–1895) was born into slavery. As was the case of many slaves, his exact birth date—even the year—was not recorded. When he was a young boy, the sister-in-law of one of his owners recognized his intelligence and began to teach him how to read. Because it was believed that if slaves could read they would want to be free, it was illegal to educate them. But Frederick continued to learn from the white children in his neighborhood and began reading newspapers and books and anything else he could get his hands on.

As a young man, Frederick was owned by a number of men, many who were extremely abusive. He attempted escape many times and was beaten severely when caught. His final escape attempt succeeded with the help of Anna Murray, a free black woman who soon became his wife. Frederick changed his last name—first to Johnson, then to Douglass—to avoid being discovered and returned to slavery.

Frederick Douglass went on to become the most important black American leader of the 1800s. A brilliant man, he became an abolitionist, writer, and public speaker. His three autobiographies contain such elegant prose that they are considered some of the finest examples of the slave narrative tradition and classics of American autobiography.

Illustrated and hand-lettered by Jennifer Tucker

"We the People of the United States, in Order to form a more perfect Union, establish Justice, insure domestic Tranquility, provide for the common defence, promote the general Welfare, and secure the Blessings of Liberty to ourselves and our Posterity, do ordain and establish this Constitution for the United States of America." —Preamble to the US Constitution

The Constitution of the United States was signed in convention in 1787 and ratified on June 21, 1788. The Constitution is the supreme law of our nation. It is the source—and the limitation—of all government powers, and it provides and protects fundamental rights of US citizens.

Illustrated by Joseph Marsh

"Far better it is to dare mighty things, to win glorious triumphs, even though checkered by failure, than to take rank with those poor spirits who neither enjoy much nor suffer much, because they live in the gray twilight that knows neither victory nor defeat."
—President Teddy Roosevelt

Theodore Roosevelt Jr., better known as Teddy Roosevelt (1858–1919), served as president from 1901 to 1909. Appointed after the assassination of William McKinley, Roosevelt was the youngest person to serve as president.

Roosevelt's favorite saying, "Speak softly and carry a big stick," characterized his foreign policy: strive for peace but let others know of your strong military capabilities.

His domestic agenda was called "Square Deal" and consisted of the three C's: conservation of natural resources, control of corporations, and consumer protection. Roosevelt was considered the first environmental president. By signing the National Monuments Act, he ensured the protection and preservation of the Grand Canyon and other significant sites including wildlife sanctuaries, national forests, and federal game reserves.

Because Teddy wasn't happy with the presidency of his successor, William Taft, he launched a third party, the Progressive Party, in order to run in the 1912 election. During one of his campaign speeches, Teddy was shot in the chest in an assassination attempt. Amazingly, he continued his speech for another hour and a half before seeking medical assistance. That election was ultimately won by Woodrow Wilson.

Teddy Roosevelt is one of the four presidents whose image is carved into Mount Rushmore.

Illustrated by Katherine Howe

America was not built on fear.

~ Harry S. Truman

"As the year 1947 opens America has never been so strong or so prosperous. Nor have our prospects ever been brighter.

"Yet in the minds of a great many of us there is a fear of another depression, the loss of our jobs, our farms, our businesses.

"But America was not built on fear. America was built on courage, on imagination and an unbeatable determination to do the job at hand.

"The job at hand today is to see to it that America is not ravaged by recurring depressions and long periods of unemployment, but that instead we build an economy so fruitful, so dynamic, so progressive that each citizen can count upon opportunity and security for himself and his family." —President Harry S. Truman in his first economic report to Congress on January 8, 1947

Harry S. Truman (1884–1972) was the vice presidential running mate with President Franklin D. Roosevelt. On April 12, 1945—eighty-two days after being sworn in as vice president—Truman was sworn in as the thirty-third president of the United States upon the unexpected death of Roosevelt. Along with the office, Truman inherited a host of wartime problems that he hadn't been fully informed about, including the development of the atomic bomb and mounting issues with the Soviet Union.

Truman's most controversial decision as president was his approval of dropping the atomic bombs on Hiroshima and Nagasaki in an effort to end the war, just four months after he took office. Within the next two months, Truman signed the charter ratifying the United Nations.

After World War II, Truman's administration focused on containing Communism. However, deteriorating relations with the Soviet Union resulted in the Cold War, beginning in 1946. On March 12, 1947, in an effort to prevent the spread of Communism, President Truman asked Congress to approve funding for political, military, and economic assistance for Greece and Turkey and establish what is known as the Truman Doctrine. The Truman Doctrine allowed for US assistance to all democratic nations threatened by authoritarian forces, whether internal or external. Truman said, "It must be the policy of the United States to support free peoples who are resisting attempted subjugation by armed minorities or by outside pressures." The Truman Doctrine ended American isolationism and signaled America's post-war embrace of global leadership.

Illustrated and hand-lettered by Holly Camp

Each person must live their life as a model for others.

—Rosa Parks

"Each person must live their life as a model
for others." —Rosa Parks

On December 1, 1955, when black seamstress Rosa Parks (1913–2005) was asked by a bus driver in Montgomery, Alabama, to give up her seat to a white man, she refused. The driver called the police, and Parks was arrested for violating the city's segregation laws.

On the day that she was convicted, a boycott against public transportation was launched by black leaders, most notably Martin Luther King Jr. The Montgomery bus boycott that lasted for over a year captured the attention of the world and was one of the nation's most successful protests against racial segregation. The boycott didn't end until the US Supreme Court ruled in November 1956 that bus segregation was unconstitutional.

As a result of her peaceful protest against segregation, Parks became known as the "Mother of the Civil Rights Movement."

Illustrated by Lisa Shirk

I am still determined to be cheerful and to be happy in whatever situation I may be.

—Martha Washington

"I am still determined to be cheerful and to be happy in whatever situation I may be, for I have also learnt from experience that the greater part of our unhappiness or misery depends upon our dispositions, and not upon our circumstances." —Martha Washington, in a letter to Mercy Otis Warren, December 26, 1789

During the long Revolutionary War, Martha Dandridge Custis Washington (1731–1802) joined her husband, George Washington—commander of the Continental Army—in his winter quarters every year and helped entertain his officers and guests. Mrs. Washington aided in the war efforts by nursing sick and wounded soldiers and raising money for the troops.

When George was elected the nation's first president in 1789, Martha became the nation's first First Lady, a job she did not particularly enjoy because of the rigid protocol. She was thankful when George's presidential term came to an end and they could retire to their Mount Vernon home (shown in the illustration). Both George and Martha are buried on the estate grounds.

Illustrated by Melinda B. Shiflet

IT TAKES A HERO
TO BE ONE OF THOSE MEN
WHO GOES INTO BATTLE.

—GENERAL NORMAN SCHWARZKOPF

"It doesn't take a hero to order men into battle. It takes a hero to be one of those men who goes into battle." —Norman Schwarzkopf

General Norman Schwarzkopf (1934–2012), nicknamed "Stormin' Norman" for his explosive temper, led Operation Desert Storm, a coalition of over thirty countries organized by President George H. W. Bush. He and his troops successfully drove out Saddam Hussein's forces to liberate Kuwait in less than six weeks in 1991.

Illustrated by Christina J. Culver

"United we stand, divided we fall. Let us not split into factions which must destroy that union upon which our existence hangs." —Patrick Henry in his final speech, March 4, 1799

Founding Father Patrick Henry (1736–1799) was a firm believer in individual liberty and freedom of speech. A gifted orator, he was known for his rousing speeches and strong support for American revolution against the British. He was elected to the First Continental Congress, where he adamantly opposed the importation of British goods. In 1775, with war looming with Great Britain, Patrick Henry gave his famous "Give me liberty or give me death!" speech (without using any written notes) to the Second Virginia Convention, pleading that the colonists should form an organized militia to fight against the advancing British troops.

Illustrated and hand-lettered by Bridget Hurley

"My dream is of a place and a time where America will once again be seen as the last best hope of earth." —President Abraham Lincoln

Abraham Lincoln (1809–1865), the sixteenth president, is considered one of the greatest presidents in history, despite the challenges he faced. Between election day in November 1860 and his inauguration in early 1861, seven Southern slave states had seceded from the Union and formed the Confederate States of America. Lincoln firmly believed that secession was illegal, and he was determined to hold the Union together. On April 12, 1861, the South fired the first shots of war at Fort Sumter, South Carolina, and the brutal, bloody Civil War began.

On January 1, 1863, halfway through the Civil War, Lincoln issued the Emancipation Proclamation, which freed all slaves in rebellious states and paved the way for the eventual abolition of slavery.

In Lincoln's inauguration speech for his second term of office, he proclaimed his desire for peace. Just over a month later, on April 14, 1865, Lincoln was assassinated at Ford's Theatre in Washington, DC, by Confederate sympathizer John Wilkes Booth.

Illustrated by Deborah Gregg

peace and friendship with all mankind is our wisest policy

—THOMAS JEFFERSON

"Peace and friendship with all mankind is our wisest policy and I wish we may be permitted to pursue it."
—Thomas Jefferson, in a letter from France to diplomat C. W. F. Dumas on May 6, 1789

Thomas Jefferson succeeded Benjamin Franklin as minister to France in 1785, where he negotiated loans and trade agreements. When he returned to the United States four years later, George Washington immediately appointed him the first Secretary of State. He served in that role for four years, until quarrels with Secretary of Treasury Alexander Hamilton caused him to resign. He was then elected president in 1800 and served until 1809.

Illustrated and hand-lettered by Jennifer Tucker

"That's one small step for man; one giant leap for mankind." —Neil Armstrong

Americans heard these words on July 20, 1969, from Apollo 11 astronaut Neil Armstrong (1930–2012), as he stepped onto the surface of the moon—the first person ever to do so.

Armstrong's lunar walk was a key victory for the United States in the space race, a rivalry that began in the 1950s between Cold War adversaries, the United States and the Soviet Union. The two countries had been battling for supremacy in spaceflight capability since the Soviet launch in the mid-1950s of Sputnik, the first artificial satellite.

Armstrong's spacewalk also fulfilled President John F. Kennedy's 1961 vision of landing a man on the moon and returning him safely to Earth by the end of the decade.

Illustration by Joseph Marsh

"We hold these truths to be self-evident, that all men are created equal, that they are endowed by their Creator with certain unalienable Rights, that among these are Life, Liberty and the pursuit of Happiness. — That to secure these rights, Governments are instituted among Men, deriving their just powers from the consent of the governed, — That whenever any Form of Government becomes destructive of these ends, it is the Right of the People to alter or to abolish it, and to institute new Government, laying its foundation on such principles and organizing its powers in such form, as to them shall seem most likely to effect their Safety and Happiness. Prudence, indeed, will dictate that Governments long established should not be changed for light and transient causes; and accordingly all experience hath shewn that mankind are more disposed to suffer, while evils are sufferable than to right themselves by abolishing the forms to which they are accustomed. But when a long train of abuses and usurpations, pursuing invariably the same Object evinces a design to reduce them under absolute Despotism, it is their right, it is their duty, to throw off such Government, and to provide new Guards for their future security. — Such has been the patient sufferance of these Colonies; and such is now the necessity which constrains them to alter their former Systems of Government. The history of the present King of Great Britain is a history of repeated injuries and usurpations, all having in direct object the establishment of an absolute Tyranny over these States." —from the Declaration of Independence

In June 1776, five men—Thomas Jefferson, John Adams, Benjamin Franklin, Roger Sherman, and Robert R. Livingston—were appointed to draft a formal statement of the colonies' intentions to sever ties with British rule. Congress formally adopted the Declaration of Independence, written largely by Jefferson, on July 4. The fourth of July is now celebrated as Independence Day.

Illustrated and hand-lettered by Lisa Shirk

we have
abundant reason
to rejoice

-GEORGE WASHINGTON-

"We have abundant reason to rejoice, that, in this land, the light of truth and reason has triumphed over the power of bigotry and superstition, and that every person may here worship God according to the dictates of his own heart." —President George Washington in a letter to the members of The New Church in Baltimore, 1793

On April 30, 1789, by a unanimous decision, George Washington (1732–1799) became the first president of our country. He is the only president in US history to receive every electoral vote.

George Washington was a man of integrity. His Secretary of State, Thomas Jefferson, wrote of him, "His integrity was most pure, his justice the most inflexible I have ever known, no motives of interest or consanguinity, of friendship or hatred, being able to bias his decision. He was indeed, in every sense of the words, a wise, a good, and a great man."

He planned on serving only a single term in office, but Jefferson encouraged him to accept a second term. Washington reluctantly agreed. Upon retirement, he and his wife, Martha, returned to their family home, Mount Vernon, where George died from illness in December 1799.

Illustrated and hand-lettered by Jennifer Tucker

"I pledge allegiance to the Flag of the United States of America, and to the Republic for which it stands, one Nation under God, indivisible, with liberty and justice for all." —Pledge of Allegiance

The US Flag Code states that the Pledge of Allegiance "should be rendered by standing at attention facing the flag with the right hand over the heart. When not in uniform men should remove any non-religious headdress with their right hand and hold it at the left shoulder, the hand being over the heart. Persons in uniform should remain silent, face the flag, and render the military salute."

Originally, the pledge was said with the right hand extended straight out at chest height in what was called the Bellamy Salute. However, when Hitler came in to power in Europe, many Americans feared this was too similar to the Nazi salute. In 1942, the US Flag Code established the current practice of saying the pledge with the right hand over the heart.

The Flag Code can be altered only by the president of the United States.

Illustrated and hand-lettered by Holly Camp

Artists, Illustrators, and Hand-Letterers

We'd like to thank the following people for sharing their creativity on the pages of this book. We handed them the text and set them free to illustrate in whatever style they chose. As you can see, there are as many styles presented as there are artists! Be sure to check out their websites and Etsy stores to see more of their artwork and to learn more about them.

Holly Camp (HollyCampCards.Etsy.com)
Christina J. Culver (Facebook.com/AllAboutTheGrain)
Deborah Gregg (ChicorySkies.com)
Katherine Howe (KatiesInkyInspirations.Wordpress.com)
Bridget Hurley (BlueSkyBeads.Etsy.com)
Joseph Marsh (TheCreativeJoe.Wordpress.com)
Melinda B. Shiflet (PrintsCardsEtc.Etsy.com)
Lisa Shirk (LisaShirk.com)
Jennifer Tucker (LittleHouseStudio.net)

Multnomah

Thank you to all of the individuals and departments within the Crown Division and Multnomah for their help in creating this project—in particular Lori Addicott, Laura Barker, Candice Chaplin, Tina Constable, Christine Edwards, Alex Field, Pam Fogle, Bridget Givan, Ginia Hairston Croker, Debbie Mitchell, Derek Reed, Andrew Rein, Beverly Rykerd, Sara Selkirk, Pam Shoup, and Julia Wallace. A very special thank you to Karen Sherry for her time and talent in the design and typesetting process.

God Bless America Development Team

Kendall Davis
Jessica Gingrich
Kristopher Orr
Susan Tjaden
Kimberly Von Fange

Playlist

To create a multisensory experience with God Bless America, we've constructed a playlist of songs to listen to while you color. Go to https://open.spotify.com/user/waterbrookmultnomah and select the playlist "Coloring America." Enjoy!

Other Resources

Visit ColoringAmerica.net for a history quiz based on what you've read in *God Bless America* and for other resources on how to include patriotism in your everyday life!